Table of Contents

Parent and family involvement has been a priority of National PTA since its founding. For more than 100 years, National PTA has consistently demonstrated that effectively involving parents and families in support of children and their education produces meaningful and lasting results.

In the midst of ongoing education reform, National PTA maintains what numerous research studies and years of experience as advocates for children have demonstrated to be true: **Parent and family involvement increases student success.**

The overall importance of parent and family involvement in education reform warrants the same consideration and attention as other areas for which national standards have been developed. Therefore, the implementation of standards that guide parents, teachers, principals, and other education leaders as they work to develop quality parent involvement programs is crucial.

Building upon the six types of parent involvement identified by Joyce L. Epstein, Ph.D., of the Center on School, Family, and Community Partnerships at Johns Hopkins University, National PTA developed standards in cooperation with other education and parent involvement organizations. The *National Standards for Parent/Family Involvement Programs* should be used in conjunction with other national standards and reform initiatives in support of children's learning and success.

> "The evidence is now beyond dispute. When parents are involved their children do better in school."
>
> — Henderson and Berla

To help school communities better understand how to use the standards to create quality parent involvement programs, in 2000 National PTA authored *Building Successful Partnerships: A Guide for Developing Parent and Family Involvement Programs* and launched the Building Successful Partnerships training program. The program prepares PTA leaders nationwide to give presentations on all facets of parent involvement, thus increasing both awareness and implementation of the standards. The results of these efforts have been impressive. Since their original publication in 1997, the standards have been endorsed by nearly 100 education, health, and parent involvement organizations; adopted in school districts across the country; supported by state departments of education; and incorporated into education legislation in numerous states.

National PTA, throughout its history, has also worked tirelessly with U.S. legislators to include parent involvement requirements in federal education laws. National PTA worked with Congress to initiate the PARENT Act in 1999. This legislation sought to strengthen the parent participation policies in the Elementary and Secondary Education Act (ESEA), our nation's largest and most comprehensive federal education law. ESEA, also known as the No Child Left Behind Act, authorizes more than 40 programs that provide federal funds to nearly every school district in the nation. This law now includes many of the parent involvement provisions of the PARENT Act and defines the term "parent involvement" based on National PTA's National Standards for Parent/Family Involvement Programs.

It is with these achievements in mind that National PTA encourages parents, teachers, principals, and all partners in education to support and implement these National Standards for Parent/Family Involvement Programs, so that student success can soar—in school and beyond.

Linda Hodge, National PTA President, 2003–2005
Anna Weselak, National PTA President-Elect, 2003–2005
Shirley Igo, National PTA President, 2001–2003

National Standards for Parent/Family Involvement Programs

Standard I: Communicating—Communication between home and school is regular, two-way, and meaningful.

Standard II: Parenting—Parenting skills are promoted and supported.

Standard III: Student Learning—Parents play an integral role in assisting student learning.

Standard IV: Volunteering—Parents are welcome in the school, and their support and assistance are sought.

Standard V: School Decision Making and Advocacy—Parents are full partners in the decisions that affect children and families.

Standard VI: Collaborating with Community—Community resources are used to strengthen schools, families, and student learning.

Benefits of Parent/Family Involvement

More than 35 years of research has proven beyond dispute the positive connection between parent* involvement and student success. Effectively engaging parents and families in the education of their children has the potential to be far more transformational than any other type of education reform. National PTA recognizes that schools with well-structured, quality parent involvement programs experience profound benefits for students, parents, teachers, and overall school quality. Here are just a few examples:

For students

- Higher grades, test scores, and graduation rates
- Better school attendance
- Greater enrollment in postsecondary education

For teachers and administrators

- Greater morale
- Increased teacher effectiveness
- Greater job satisfaction

For parents

- Improved communication with teachers
- Increased education skills
- Improved attitude toward school and school personnel

Throughout this document are references to "parent" involvement. All such references may be interpreted broadly to include the adults who play an important role in a child's family life, since other adults—grandparents, aunts, uncles, step-parents, guardians—may carry the primary responsibility for a child's education, development, and well-being.

Purpose of This Guide

This guide was developed to be a practical tool for schools* to use to

- Promote meaningful parent and family participation
- Raise awareness regarding the components of effective programs
- Provide guidelines for schools that wish to evaluate and improve their programs

The booklet can be used by school administrators, teachers, parents, and other community members to improve programs serving parents and families. It can direct these groups as they move from discussion to action in developing dynamic programs to improve student achievement through parent involvement. As with any effective long-term reform, the overall integration and implementation of all of the standards should be tailored to meet the local needs and circumstances of individual school communities.

Throughout this document are references to "schools." All such references may be interpreted broadly to include other programs that serve children and families, i.e., other academic, specialty, or community programs.

Special Features of This Guide

This guide was designed as an interactive tool to facilitate **discussion, planning, and assessment** of parent/family involvement programs. Therefore, the following special features have been included to meet these objectives.

- **Research findings.** The research that led to the development of the *National Standards for Parent/Family Involvement Programs* is summarized in this section. The findings provide insight into how parent and family involvement is directly linked to student success, quality schools, and effective reform strategies. They can be used in communications and presentations to parents and community members about the importance of parent involvement in education.

> The booklet can be used by school administrators, teachers, parents, and other community members to improve programs serving parents and families.

- **Assessment questions.** Beginning on page 12, each of the six program standards is defined and accompanied by a series of questions schools can use to evaluate their current parent involvement practices. The questions identify the important elements of each standard that need to be in place if unique gains are to be realized. They inform schools about what contributes to effective programs and fosters success. Each set of assessment questions can be used individually to identify strengths as well as weaknesses in a particular standard area. The assessment as a whole can be used to evaluate the overall quality of a school's parent involvement program.

The six sections of assessment questions presented in this guide are just a part of a comprehensive process National PTA has developed to help schools evaluate and gain recognition for their parent involvement efforts: National PTA's **Parent Involvement Schools of Excellence Certification.** Applying for certification presents a unique opportunity for a school community to come together to learn, grow, and develop its parent involvement programs. To learn more about National PTA's Parent Involvement Schools of Excellence Certification, go to page 10.

- **Action ideas.** Benefits for students are greatest when parents participate in activities in each of the six standard areas; therefore, examples for putting ideas into action accompany each program standard.

- **Voices from the field.** Parent Involvement Schools of Excellence from across the country provide information on how they have implemented a particular standard.

- **Steps toward developing parent/family involvement programs.** This special section features information on developing a parent/family involvement policy and plan with **reproducible tear-out sheets** for your team to use to create a policy and plan tailored to your school. A ready-made survey to distribute to parents and a publications order form are also included.

- **Additional resources**

  —**PTA project ideas.** Ideas for PTAs to use to help schools implement each standard effectively.

  —**Bibliography.** A list of current and relevant studies to be used by parents, teachers, and administrators as they research parent involvement program development.

A list of all of the supporters of the national standards begins on page 46. Nearly 100 education, health, and parent involvement organizations have endorsed the standards.

Research Findings on Parent/Family Involvement

The most comprehensive survey of the research is a series of publications developed by Anne Henderson and Nancy Berla: *The Evidence Grows* (1981); *The Evidence Continues to Grow* (1987); and *A New Generation of Evidence: The Family Is Critical to Student Achievement* (1995). Citing more than 85 studies, these publications document the profound and comprehensive benefits for students, families, and schools, when parents and family members become participants in their children's education and their lives.

The latest addition to the series, *A New Wave of Evidence: The Impact of School, Family, and Community Connections on Student Achievement* (2002), examines the impact of various family and community connections on student achievement. Authors Anne Henderson and Karen Mapp reviewed more than 50 research studies published since 1995 to build an ever-strengthening case to show that families have a major influence on their children's achievement in school and throughout life.

The findings below are from the empirical research.

> "When schools, families, and community groups work together to support learning, children tend to do better in school, stay in school longer, and like school more."
>
> — Henderson and Mapp

Findings on Student Achievement

- Programs that engage families in supporting their children's learning at home are linked to higher student achievement.

- When parents are involved, students achieve more, regardless of socioeconomic status, ethnic/racial background, or the parents' education level.

- When parents are involved in their students' education, those students have higher grades and test scores, better attendance, and complete homework more consistently.

- Students whose parents are involved in their lives have higher graduation rates and greater enrollment rates in postsecondary education.

- In programs that are designed to involve parents in full partnerships, student achievement for disadvantaged children not only improves, it can reach levels that are standard for middle-class children.

- Students are more likely to fall behind in academic performance if their parents do not participate in school events, develop a working relationship with their child's educators, or keep up with what is happening in their child's school.

Findings on Student Behavior

- When parents are involved, students exhibit more positive attitudes and behavior.

- When students report feeling support from both home and school, they have more self-confidence, feel school is more important, and they tend to do better in school.

- Student behaviors such as alcohol use, violence, and other antisocial behaviors decrease as parent involvement increases.

Findings on Culture

- Children from diverse cultural backgrounds tend to do better when parents and professionals collaborate to bridge the gap between the culture at home and the culture at school.

- The school's practices to inform and involve parents are stronger determinants of whether inner-city parents will be involved with their children's education than are parent education, family size, marital status, and even student grade level.

- Successful schools are those that succeed in engaging families from very diverse backgrounds, focus on building trusting collaborative relationships among teachers, families, and community members; recognize, respect, and address families' needs, as well as class and cultural differences; and embrace a philosophy of partnership where power and responsibility are shared.

- For low-income families, programs offered in the community, at church, or those that include home visits are more successful in involving parents than programs that require parents to visit the school. However, when parents become involved at school, their children make even greater gains.

Findings on Age

- The benefits of involving parents are not confined to the early years; there are significant gains at all ages and grade levels.

- Junior and senior high school students whose parents remain involved are able to make better transitions, maintain the quality of their work, and develop realistic plans for their futures. Students whose parents are not involved, on the other hand, are more likely to drop out of school.

Findings on School Quality

- Schools that have parent-teacher groups have higher student achievement than schools that do not.

- Schools that work well with families have improved teacher morale and higher ratings of teachers by parents.

- When parents and community members organize to hold poorly performing schools accountable, school districts make positive changes in policy and practice that lead to upgraded school facilities, improved school leadership and staffing, new resources for programs to improve teaching and curriculum, and funding for after school and family support programs.

- Schools where parents are involved have more support from families and better reputations in the community.

- Schools with highly rated parent partnership programs make greater gains on state tests than schools with lower rated programs.

Parent Involvement Schools of Excellence Certification

National PTA's Parent Involvement Schools of Excellence Certification was designed to assist every school in this nation to evaluate and increase its parent involvement practices. Certification recognizes schools that have worked to create and enhance parent involvement programs based on the *National Standards for Parent/Family Involvement Programs.* Therefore, when schools receive certification, they will be recognized as upholding the highest standards in parent involvement.

All schools have the opportunity to earn one of two distinctions: **Certification of Excellence,** awarded to schools that have outstanding parent involvement practices in place and **Recognition of Commitment,** given to schools that are committed to pursuing excellence in parent involvement.

School certification provides many benefits to a community. The process of participating in certification is a unique opportunity for a school community to come together to learn and grow. Throughout the certification process a school team works to discuss and evaluate its efforts and discover areas that need strengthening. Certification can be used in a school's public relations efforts to gain recognition and respect for the school and can be used in support of grant applications. It also aids in teacher recruitment—a strong parent involvement program can make a school attractive to quality teachers.

Every child deserves to attend a school of excellence. Schools interested in moving through the process of certification can go online at www.pta.org/parentinvolvement/certification/.

"Even though the Schools of Excellence Committee recognized that Paxtonia Elementary School already had excellent parent involvement practices, it was still enlightening to learn more about what administrators do, teachers do, how the community looks at schools, and just what parents are thinking. We became better acquainted with what resources are available to parents and teachers. We made a commitment to improve the parent/teacher resource center, [and] to try to track the number of volunteer hours that are given to Paxtonia. We will strive for continued excellence in public education and parent involvement practices."

—Paxtonia Elementary School, Harrisburg, Pennsylvania

The Standards

This section presents the six standards for parent/family involvement and their accompanying definitions. Following each standard's definition are the **assessment questions** for determining how effectively that standard is implemented in your school and a rating scale to rate your school's accomplishment in each assessed area. Schools can review their ratings to determine what, if any, action they need to take to improve their activity in that standard. They then can use the parent involvement plan template on page 30 to develop activities to enhance that standard. Examples of possible activities (action ideas beginning on page 13 and PTA project ideas beginning on page 38) are included to help in developing the plan.

Standard I: Communicating

Standard II: Parenting

Standard III: Student Learning

Standard IV: Volunteering

Standard V: School Decision Making and Advocacy

Standard VI: Collaborating with Community

Standard I. Communicating

Communication between home and school is regular, two-way, and meaningful.

Communication is the foundation of a solid partnership. When parents and educators communicate effectively, positive relationships develop, problems are more easily solved, and students make greater progress.

Too often, school or program communication is *one-way* without the chance to exchange ideas and share perceptions. Effective home-school communication is the *two-way* sharing of information vital to student success. Even parent-teacher conferences can be one-way if the goal is merely reporting student progress. A strong parent-teacher partnership requires give-and-take conversation, goal setting for the future, and regular follow-up interactions.

Rating Scale: Check off how your school rates in each area.

Excellent: Activity occurs each year and is consistently implemented throughout the school year.
Good: Activity occurs sometimes during the school year, but is not consistently practiced.
Fair: Activity occurs rarely during the school year.
Poor: Activity does not occur at the school.

Assessment Questions Does the school:	Excellent	Good	Fair	Poor
1. Communicate with parents in a variety of ways (e.g., newsletter, e-mail, home visits, phone calls)?	☐	☐	☐	☐
2. Provide information to parents in a language and format they can understand?	☐	☐	☐	☐
3. Conduct conferences with parents that accommodate needs such as the varied schedules of parents, language translations, and child care?	☐	☐	☐	☐
4. Encourage parents and educators to share information such as student strengths and learning preferences during parent-teacher conferences?	☐	☐	☐	☐
5. Provide clear information regarding school policies and procedures?	☐	☐	☐	☐
6. Discuss student report cards with parents?	☐	☐	☐	☐
7. Disseminate information on topics such as school reforms, policies, discipline procedures, assessment tools, and school goals?	☐	☐	☐	☐
8. Encourage immediate contact between parents and teachers when concerns arise?	☐	☐	☐	☐
9. Distribute student work for parental review on a regular basis?	☐	☐	☐	☐
10. Communicate with parents regarding positive student behavior and achievement, not just regarding misbehavior or failure?	☐	☐	☐	☐
11. Promote informal activities at which parents, staff, the principal, and community members can interact?	☐	☐	☐	☐
12. Provide staff development regarding effective communication techniques and the importance of regular, two-way communication between the school and the family?	☐	☐	☐	☐
13. Use technology (e.g., telephone hotline, translation equipment, e-mail, website) to foster communication with parents?	☐	☐	☐	☐

Action Ideas

Following are some ideas for implementing Standard I.

- Create a welcoming environment for parents. Place large signs welcoming all visitors at all school entrances and on each classroom door written in all the major languages spoken in the school. Consider using color-coded lines on hallway walls or footprints on floors to help direct parents to important places like the office, parent center, or library.

- Explore program and community support options for improving mail, telephone, fax, or e-mail access and use for educators and parents. For example, automated phone systems, such as a telephone hotline, are powerful tools for getting information to parents—from daily assignments and attendance reports to parenting tips and student achievement information.

- Create class or program newsletters for parents that contain tips for helping children learn in the home, fun activities to do as a family, and other useful ideas.

- Establish a routine method for parents to review their children's work on a regular basis. For example, use manila envelopes or folders to send student work home each week with a place for parent comments on the front cover.

- Implement additional feedback opportunities for parents and family members such as surveys on current program issues or special parent guest columns in the school newsletter.

- Sponsor program or community events that allow educators and parents to interact on a social basis in addition to standard parent-teacher conferences or school/program meetings.

Voices from the Field

"Examples of communication at **J. L. Mann High School** in Greenville, South Carolina, are monthly PTSA newsletters mailed home, weekly e-mail newsletters, 'special announcement' automated phone messages to all students, and our school website. In order to facilitate two-way communication, translators are offered for conferences with parents of different languages or for those who cannot read. A Spanish translation of the PTSA newsletter is now being offered to the Spanish population. Home visits, visits to the workplace, or conference calls are offered to parents who cannot come to school. Faculty communications with families include 'Good News' postcards, notes written on report cards, and e-mail messages."

J. L. Mann High School Team
Greenville, SC

"**Livsey School (Pre-K–6)** in Tucker, Georgia, communicates through a wide variety of print materials, state-of-the-art technology, and personal interaction. A monthly newsletter, school handbook, school directory, and weekly courier packs provide information about school activities and policies, while conduct reports and progress reports/report cards show student progress. Parent-teacher conferences, PTA meetings, school council meetings, and social events provide opportunities for dialogue between parents and teachers. E-mail, voice mail, phone calls, and the Livsey Web page provide additional communication links. Livsey reaches out to international families by providing translators and translations [of school materials]."

Livsey Elementary School Team
Tucker, GA

Standard II. Parenting

Parenting skills are promoted and supported.

Parents are a child's life support system. Consequently, the most important support a child can receive comes from the home.

School personnel and program staff support positive parenting by respecting and affirming the strengths and skills needed by parents to fulfill their role. From making sure that students arrive at school rested, nourished, and ready to learn, to setting high learning expectations and nurturing self-esteem, parents sustain their children's learning.

When staff members recognize parent roles and responsibilities, ask what support parents need, and work to find ways to meet those needs, they communicate a clear message to parents: "We value you and need your input" in order to maintain a high-quality program.

Rating Scale: Check off how your school rates in each area.

Excellent: Activity occurs each year and is consistently implemented throughout the school year.
Good: Activity occurs sometimes during the school year, but is not consistently practiced.
Fair: Activity occurs rarely during the school year.
Poor: Activity does not occur at the school.

Assessment Questions Does the school:	Excellent	Good	Fair	Poor
1. Communicate the importance of positive relationships between parents and their children?	☐	☐	☐	☐
2. Link parents to family support services and resources in the community?	☐	☐	☐	☐
3. Share information on parenting issues with all families by including information on the school's website, hotline, and/or newsletter?	☐	☐	☐	☐
4. Establish school policies that recognize and respect families' cultural and religious diversity?	☐	☐	☐	☐
5. Provide an accessible parent/family information and resource center?	☐	☐	☐	☐
6. Work with PTAs, parent educators, or other community groups to host on-site meetings?	☐	☐	☐	☐

Action Ideas

Following are some ideas for implementing Standard II.

- Find out which ethnic groups are represented in each school or program. Provide translation and other support services when needed. Be sensitive to cultural differences, and find appropriate ways to communicate acceptance and respect.

- Consult parents prior to providing special services for children such as counseling or other social services.

- At least once a year, schedule a school or program event with workshops given by professional personnel or local parent educators to help parents deal with parenting issues. Provide child care and transportation to encourage parents and family members to participate.

- Develop "family kits" built around relevant themes with games, videos, conversation starters, or other tools for parents to interact with their children on a specific topic. For example, a kit could be built around the theme of setting family goals or developing house rules.

Voices from the Field

"**Albion Elementary** in North Royalton, Ohio, does an excellent job of supporting parents. Each year the guidance counselors from the three elementary buildings in our district, including Albion, jointly host a series of parenting workshops. Child care is also provided free of charge so that the workshop is accessible to all. Albion PTA organizes family breakfasts at the school in order to foster positive family relationships between students and parents. When staff becomes aware of a family situation requiring community support, the principal or guidance counselor is notified and appropriate contacts are made. The office maintains an information center and parenting tips are offered by the guidance counselor in the monthly PTA newsletter. Cultural and religious diversity is respected through holiday music programs that focus on a variety of backgrounds."

> Albion Elementary School Team
> North Royalton, OH

"Parenting skills at **Yankton Middle School** (YMS) in Yankton, South Dakota, are reinforced by the guidance office and the administration, the PTSA newsletter, the YMS and district websites, community parenting classes, and the Mentor Mom Program. We sponsor and host speakers throughout the year that address parenting concerns. Some of the recent topics include inhalant use, eating disorders, and methadone use. YMS has a nondiscrimination policy and works closely with families to recognize and respect their cultural differences. Lunch menus provide a non-meat substitute and provisions are made for Ramadan [a Muslim holy month] observances. Native American Day (observed in South Dakota on Columbus Day), is incorporated into all curriculum and culminates with a Wacipi celebration. Parents are encouraged to make their cultural needs known."

> Yankton Middle School Team
> Yankton, SD

Respecting Diverse Family Cultures and Traditions

Quality schools and programs must be culturally sensitive to increasingly diverse student and family populations. Appreciating the traditions of families from various cultures requires, first of all, an awareness and acceptance of their differences.

Find ways to help parents and families value and share their distinctiveness. Cultural fairs or other opportunities to celebrate specific ethnic holidays or traditions may help parents and family members develop a sense of belonging and ownership in the school and community. Making resources available in the parents' first language remains critical in responding to the needs and concerns of the parents and families served.

Standard III. Student Learning

Parents play an integral role in assisting student learning.

Student learning increases when parents are invited into the process by helping at home. Enlisting parents' involvement provides educators and administrators with a valuable support system—creating a team that is working for each child's success.

The vast majority of parents are willing to assist their students in learning, but many times are not sure what assistance is most helpful and appropriate. Helping parents connect to their children's learning enables parents to communicate in powerful ways that they value what their children achieve. Whether it's working together on a computer, displaying student work at home, or responding to a particular class assignment, parents' actions communicate to their children that education is important.

Rating Scale: Check off how your school rates in each area.

Excellent: Activity occurs each year and is consistently implemented throughout the school year.
Good: Activity occurs sometimes during the school year, but is not consistently practiced.
Fair: Activity occurs rarely during the school year.
Poor: Activity does not occur at the school.

Assessment Questions Does the school:	Excellent	Good	Fair	Poor
1. Provide clear information regarding the expectations for students in each subject at each grade level, as well as information regarding student placement, student services, and optional programs?	☐	☐	☐	☐
2. Regularly assign homework that requires students to discuss and interact with their parents about what they are learning?	☐	☐	☐	☐
3. Assist parents in understanding how students can improve skills, get help when needed, meet class expectations, and perform well on assessments?	☐	☐	☐	☐
4. Involve parents in setting student goals each school year?	☐	☐	☐	☐
5. Involve parents in planning for the transition to middle school, high school, or postsecondary education and careers? (Base your answer on the type of school you are: i.e., elementary, middle/junior high, or high school.)	☐	☐	☐	☐
6. Provide opportunities for staff members to learn about successful approaches to engaging parents in their child's learning?	☐	☐	☐	☐

Action Ideas

Following are some ideas for implementing Standard III.

- Provide information sheets to guide parents in helping students with a particular skill—for example, information that explains how to help a young child with reading or how to help a teen with a research project.

- Some projects readily lend themselves to involving parents or other family members. Examples include personal interviews on specific topics, reports based on visits to community museums or points of interest, or discussing a writing assignment. Provide advance instructions and specific guidelines for each project.

- Ask parents to take an active role in reviewing student portfolios. Parents have the opportunity to review project expectations, discover their child's areas of strength, and gain insight in how to help their child improve.

- Provide brief workshops for parents and students on topics such as study skills, new information on a particular curriculum area, or college and career planning. Include hands-on learning activities.

Voices from the Field

"**W.P. Davidson High School** in Mobile, Alabama, hosts two Open Houses for parents each year. Every teacher provides parents with a class fact sheet that includes a course syllabus, objectives, projects, pacing guide, class rules and policies, teacher conference times, and other pertinent information. We have a summer orientation for freshmen parents and include information about how parents can best support their high school student. Every senior [high] parent has a private summer conference to discuss his [or her] child's senior year and transition to post–high school. From January to March, we open our guidance department four nights a week for parent conferences. We hold at least one in-service each year with staff to address successful parent relations."

W. P. Davidson High School Team
Mobile, AL

"At **Suffield Elementary School** in Mogadore, Ohio, parents play an integral role in assisting student learning. Each year as a student enters a new grade, parents are informed of the expectations of that grade level. Open house, conferences, and the Ohio Standards booklet are all opportunities for teachers to share information on how parents can help with student learning. School policy requires teachers to assign homework that involves student and parent interaction. Students have assignment books that parents must view each night and sign. Daily, parents are invited to serve as "tutors" in the classroom, run grade-learning centers, and coordinate after-school enrichment activities. Parents are invited to help students with difficulties set goals. As students progress to the middle school, parents are part of the student tour and the course selection process."

Suffield Elementary School Team
Mogadore, OH

Sample Home-to-School Communication

Design homework assignments to include parent sign-off. Provide instructions about what to look for in each assignment, and offer a quick check-off response such as

❑ My child understands and correctly applies this skill.
❑ My child needed help on this, but overall seems to understand this lesson.
❑ My child needs further instruction on this skill/lesson.

Other comments _____

_____
Parent signature

Standard IV. Volunteering

Parents are welcome in the school, and their support and assistance are sought.

When parents volunteer, both families and schools reap benefits that come in few other ways. Literally millions of dollars of volunteer services are performed by parents and family members each year in the public schools. Studies have concluded that volunteers express greater confidence in the schools where they have opportunities to participate regularly. In addition, assisting in school or program events/activities communicates to a child, "I care about what you do here."

In order for parents to feel appreciated and welcome, volunteer work must be meaningful and valuable to them. Capitalizing on the expertise and skills of parents and family members provides much-needed support to educators and administrators already taxed in their attempts to meet academic goals and student needs.

Although there are many parents for whom volunteering during school hours is not possible, creative solutions like before- or after-school "drop-in" programs or "at-home" support activities provide opportunities for parents to offer their assistance as well.

Rating Scale: **Check off how your school rates in each area.**

Excellent: Activity occurs each year and is consistently implemented throughout the school year.
Good: Activity occurs sometimes during the school year, but is not consistently practiced.
Fair: Activity occurs rarely during the school year.
Poor: Activity does not occur at the school.

Assessment Questions
Does the school:

	Excellent	Good	Fair	Poor
1. Ensure that office staff greetings, signage near the entrances, and any other interactions with parents create a climate in which parents feel valued and welcome?	☐	☐	☐	☐
2. Survey parents regarding their interests, talents, and availability to volunteer?	☐	☐	☐	☐
3. Ensure that parents who are unable to volunteer in the school building are given options to help in other ways (e.g., at home or place of employment)?	☐	☐	☐	☐
4. Provide ample training on volunteer procedures and school protocol?	☐	☐	☐	☐
5. Develop a system for contacting parents to volunteer throughout the school year?	☐	☐	☐	☐
6. Show appreciation for parent participation and contributions?	☐	☐	☐	☐
7. Educate and assist teachers to effectively use volunteer resources?	☐	☐	☐	☐
8. Match volunteer activities to volunteer interests and abilities?	☐	☐	☐	☐
9. Track volunteer hours throughout the school year?	☐	☐	☐	☐
10. Include parent involvement activities on the school's report card? (The school's report card is a document on the school's performance, created and mailed by the school or district to all parents.)	☐	☐	☐	☐

Action Ideas

Following are some ideas for implementing Standard IV.

- Develop a survey to gather parent and family volunteer information including special skills or talents. Provide opportunities for those who are able to volunteer during the day, those who are able to commit to regular service, and those who can participate occasionally at home or at work. Be sure to follow up with volunteers on a timely basis.

- Train volunteers regarding school protocol, volunteer expectations, and equipment usage. Give clear instructions for completing volunteer tasks as well as the appropriate staff or teacher contact name if more information is needed. Look for creative ways to show appreciation for volunteer support.

- Provide a consistent place and process for parent volunteers to sign in and list the hours served. In addition, provide surveys regarding school or program climate. Encourage volunteers to offer their suggestions by using "anonymous" response forms.

- Invite parents to join their child for lunch whenever convenient. If possible, provide free lunch during the year.

Voices from the Field

"The school board had to implement funding cuts which eliminated the 3rd- and 4th- grade foreign language enrichment program, known as FLES at **Linden Elementary School** in Oak Ridge, Tennessee. Approximately 20 parents mobilized and formed lunchtime Spanish classes using a video-based program funded by PTA. Staff and parents worked on the logistics, training, and site preparation in a wonderful display of cooperation. Currently, about 80 students in kindergarten through 4th grade are receiving lunchtime Spanish instruction weekly at Linden. These parents and school staff members are committed to filling an educational void left by the sad inevitability of today's tight budgetary constraints."

Linden Elementary School Team
Oak Ridge, TN

"At **Luther Jones Elementary** in Corpus Christi, Texas, everyone is a scholar! Our most significant accomplishments occurred because of this exemplary group of scholars. Parents are integral to our scholars' ability to take the knowledge gained on our campus and use it in other arenas. The success at Luther Jones, and our exemplary status, is a direct result of mentoring, modeling, and expecting every person to achieve his/her best. One of our most outstanding accomplishments is the actual number of hours our parents volunteer. We had over 300 active parent volunteers log over 8,000 volunteer hours last year! For volunteers working with scholars, this averages out to be one half-hour per week for each one of our 678 students. This means every student works with a parent volunteer at some time during each week and does not include the number of hours our parents come for conferences, activities, lunch, or just to visit."

Luther Jones Elementary School Team
Corpus Christi, TX

Standard V. School Decision Making and Advocacy

Parents are full partners in the decisions that affect children and families.

Studies have shown that schools where parents are involved in decision making and advocacy have higher levels of student achievement and greater public support.

Effective partnerships develop when each partner is respected and empowered to fully participate in the decision-making process. Schools and programs that actively enlist parent participation and input communicate that parents are valued as full partners in the educating of their children.

Parents and educators depend on shared authority in decision-making systems to foster parental trust, public confidence, and mutual support of each other's efforts in helping students succeed. The involvement of parents, as individuals or as representative of others, is crucial in collaborative decision-making processes on issues ranging from curriculum and course selection to discipline policies and overall school reform measures.

Rating Scale: Check off how your school rates in each area.

Excellent: Activity occurs each year and is consistently implemented throughout the school year.
Good: Activity occurs sometimes during the school year, but is not consistently practiced.
Fair: Activity occurs rarely during the school year.
Poor: Activity does not occur at the school.

Assessment Questions Does the school:	Excellent	Good	Fair	Poor
1. Provide workshops for parents that teach them to influence decisions, raise issues or concerns, and resolve problems?	☐	☐	☐	☐
2. Encourage the formation of PTAs or other parent groups that respond to issues of interest to parents?	☐	☐	☐	☐
3. Include and give equal representation to parents on decision-making and advisory committees?	☐	☐	☐	☐
4. Provide parents with current information regarding school policies, practices, and both student and school performance data?	☐	☐	☐	☐
5. Encourage and facilitate active parent participation in the decisions that affect students (e.g., student placement, course selection, and individual education programs [IEPs])?	☐	☐	☐	☐
6. Treat parent concerns with respect and demonstrate genuine interest in developing solutions?	☐	☐	☐	☐
7. Promote parent participation on school district, state, and national committees that focus on education issues?	☐	☐	☐	☐
8. Provide training for staff and parents in how to be collaborative partners and share decision-making in areas such as policy, curriculum, budget, school reform, safety, and personnel issues?	☐	☐	☐	☐
9. Provide parents with an opportunity to participate in professional development activities (e.g., workshops or technology training)?	☐	☐	☐	☐

Action Ideas

Following are some ideas for implementing Standard V.

- Share annual reports of school performance and program information with parents at an open meeting to review current progress and solicit input for future goals. Respect for parent perspectives fosters increased understanding of school challenges, more effective program goals for improvement, and overall increased parent and community support.

- Communicate school/program procedures for addressing parent concerns including appropriate contact person and the process for defining the problem and developing and implementing solutions. Publicize successful changes in the school or program as a result of parent initiation and involvement.

- Include a mini-poll (one question) of parent opinions in each program newsletter covering a wide range of topics over time. Use parent feedback in making school/program decisions.

- Develop workshops or include parents in ongoing training on relevant topics such as developing parents as advocates, mastering skills for supporting learning, identifying and supporting learning styles, resolving difficulties, and fostering student achievement.

Voices from the Field

"**Pawnee Elementary** in Overland Park, Kansas, has a PTA Legislative Chair who keeps everyone up-to-date on what is happening in the state legislature through e-mails and articles in the school newsletter. The school district has a legislative link on its home page and the school sponsored a "Write Your Congressman Night." City council members spoke at one of the PTA meetings. PTA is involved in giving school grants to enhance curriculum, and [PTA] members met with the principal to create a new school traffic pattern. Parents are involved in their own student's learning and decision making by attending School Improvement Team (SIT) meetings and Individual Education Program (IEP) meetings."

Pawnee Elementary School Team
Overland Park, KS

"One of **Antioch High School's** most effective decision-making bodies is that of our Leadership Committee. Every month, our principal meets with teachers, staff members, parents and student government leaders to discuss and make decisions on important and crucial school issues such as curriculum, budgetary expenditures, dress codes, and class schedules. It is a democratic forum for all sectors to discuss, investigate, and decide courses of action that affect our school community. It promotes student and parent participation and enhances the relationship within the school as well as between home and school. Our principal advocates an open-door policy of listening to and working with anyone who is interested in the welfare of our students—a major factor in [our school's] success and credibility."

Antioch High School Team
Antioch, CA

Standard VI. Collaborating with Community

Community resources are used to strengthen schools, families, and student learning.

As part of the larger community, schools and other programs fulfill important community goals. In like fashion, communities offer a wide array of resources valuable to schools and the families they serve.

When schools and communities work together, both are strengthened in synergistic ways and make gains that outpace what either entity could accomplish on its own:

- Families access community resources more easily;
- Businesses connect education programs with the realities of the workplace;
- Seniors contribute wisdom and gain a greater sense of purpose; and ultimately,
- Students serve and learn beyond their school involvement.

The best partnerships are mutually beneficial and structured to connect individuals, not just institutions or groups. This connection enables the power of community partnerships to be unleashed.

Rating Scale: Check off how your school rates in each area.

Excellent: Activity occurs each year and is consistently implemented throughout the school year.
Good: Activity occurs sometimes during the school year, but is not consistently practiced.
Fair: Activity occurs rarely during the school year.
Poor: Activity does not occur at the school.

Assessment Questions Does the school:	Excellent	Good	Fair	Poor
1. Distribute to staff and parents information on community resources that serve the cultural, recreational, academic, health, social, and other needs of families within the community?	☐	☐	☐	☐
2. Develop partnerships with local business, community organizations, and service groups to advance student learning and assist schools and families?	☐	☐	☐	☐
3. Foster student participation in community service?	☐	☐	☐	☐
4. Involve community members in school volunteer programs?	☐	☐	☐	☐
5. Disseminate information to school community members, including those without school-age children, regarding school programs and performance?	☐	☐	☐	☐
6. Collaborate with community agencies to provide family support services and adult learning opportunities, enabling parents to more fully participate in activities that support education?	☐	☐	☐	☐

Action Ideas

Following are some ideas for implementing Standard VI.

- Work with community partners to hold special events such as health fairs, technology nights, or other learning opportunities to inform parents and families of community resources and services. Community partners may include local businesses, church and civic groups and other nonprofits, and local media. Keep the events family-focused by providing activities suitable for both children and adults.

- Recruit school or program volunteers from senior citizen groups. Provide recruitment information that is highly specific about tasks to be performed, timeframe, and specific program requirements. Find creative ways to show appreciation to seniors for their assistance.

- In the local chamber of commerce newsletter, include a request from the school district superintendent for employer cooperation and encouragement of parent attendance at parent-teacher conferences and other parent involvement activities.

- Furnish local employers with information sheets containing parenting/parent involvement ideas.

Voices from the Field

"Our proudest accomplishment at **Dogwood Elementary School** in Germantown, Tennessee, would have to be the *Rainshaven Parent Partnership*. This is a cooperative effort our parents make with a local inner-city school to tutor children at Rainshaven Elementary who have fallen behind. We have a group of parents who meet at our school most mornings and drive to this school. We then proceed to work with these children throughout the morning for several hours. We do this for seven months a year. We started this program when we were told of a need in the Memphis area. We have always had an outpouring of support here in our neighborhood and in our school, but suddenly we were given an opportunity to help others less fortunate. It has been a 'win-win'!!"

Dogwood Elementary School Team
Germantown, TN

"**Jackson Elementary** in Albuquerque, New Mexico, is very involved with the community. We have several businesses as community partners. These businesses support us financially through use of their "cards" when shopping and by providing judges for our science fair, spelling bee, and cup-stacking tournament as well as tutoring in our Reading Partners program. They are kept informed through our school marquee and our school website. Many grandparents are on our e-mail [list]. Our school also gives back to the community [through efforts] such as our annual Jump-A-Thon for the American Heart Association, raising over $5,300 this year; contributing clothes and $1,000 to the APS clothing bank; the Run 4 Zoo; the canned food drive sponsored by the student council; and contributing spare change for the Ronald McDonald House."

Jackson Elementary School Team
Albuquerque, NM

Community Service Learning

More and more schools are providing students with the opportunity to learn by serving in the community. From soup kitchens and cleanup projects, to volunteer activities in government and business, these hands-on student opportunities are especially powerful when linked to class discussions and curriculum objectives.

In some cases where student skills have been linked to employer needs, employers are able to complete important projects, while students benefit from new learning experiences in actual work settings.

Steps Toward Developing Parent/Family Involvement Programs

1. **Create a school team.** Establish a permanent parent involvement committee or task force to review or revise parent/family involvement practices including the development or revision of a parent/family involvement policy and plan. Members should include teachers, administrators, parents, community members, and representatives from specialized areas of education such as bilingual, special education, and Title I. The committee should represent the diversity of the community.

2. **Examine current practice.** Use the assessment questions and rating scale for each standard on pages 12–22 to evaluate the current status of the parent involvement programs in your school. Use the Parent Survey on page 31 to get an idea of the needs of parents.

3. **Apply the findings.** Use the results of committee discussion, the parent survey, and the assessment ratings to answer the following questions: Where are we now? Where do we want to go? How can we get there? The answers to these questions will assist you in crafting the policy and plan.

4. **Develop a written parent/family involvement policy.** A written policy establishes the vision, common mission, and foundation for future plans. The committee should create a parent involvement policy. See guidelines for developing a policy on the opposite page and a policy template on page 27.

5. **Develop a parent/family involvement plan.** A parent/family involvement policy, even after adoption, cannot stand alone. To be effective the policy requires a plan for its implementation. The plan should be based on the National Standards for Parent/Family Involvement Programs and describe what activities will take place throughout the year in each standard area. See the plan template and sample on pages 29–30.

   —**Secure community support.** Widely distribute the final draft of the plan to key stakeholders—those responsible for implementation, those who will be affected, and those outside the school who have influence over outcomes. Allow sufficient time for response and reaction.

   —**Ensure success.** Once approved, publish the plan and make it readily available to the community. Hold an informational meeting to explain the plan and the policy and their meaning to the school community. Provide training to school staff on how to work together to implement the plan. Recognize and celebrate each goal and mile stone that is achieved.

   —**Evaluate and revise.** Make a commitment to modify and evaluate the plan periodically for continued success.

Guidelines for Developing a Parent/Family Involvement Policy

The process for developing policies should include input from

- Administrators
- School board members
- Business and community leaders
- Parents
- Students
- Teachers
- Other key stakeholders

Policies should be based on and include the *National Standards for Parent/Family Involvement Programs* and incorporate opportunities for parents to become involved in all standard areas. An effective policy should include elements that

- Provide opportunities for all parents to become involved in decision making about how the parent/family involvement programs will be designed, implemented, assessed, and strengthened.

- Provide outreach to encourage participation of parents who might have low-level literacy skills and/or for whom English is not their primary language.

- Inform parents regularly about the objectives of educational programs and their child's participation and progress in those programs.

- Provide professional development for teachers and staff to enhance their effectiveness with parents.

- Form links with special service agencies and community groups to address key family and community issues.

- Allow involvement of parents of children at all ages and grade levels.

- Provide opportunities for parents to share in decision making regarding school policies and procedures affecting their children.

- Recognize diverse family structures, circumstances, and responsibilities including differences that might impede parent participation. The person(s) responsible for a child may not be the child's biological parent(s), and policies and programs should include participation by all persons interested in the child's educational progress.

- Define how the policy will be implemented and enforced and what type of reporting procedure will be established with parents, the community, and the school district.

Excerpted from Developing Family/School Partnerships: Guidelines for Schools and School Districts, *National Coalition for Parent Involvement in Education.*

To learn how states and school districts around the country have used National PTA's National Standards for Parent/Family Involvement Programs to create parent involvement policies, visit the parent involvement area of National PTA's website at www.pta.org

Reproducibles to Aid in Parent/Family Involvement Program Planning

Beginning on the opposite page is a series of reproducibles, which schools can tear out and use in developing a parent/family involvement policy and plan. These include the following:

• Parent/Family Involvement Policy Template, which can be used as a model in developing a policy;

• Sample Plan and Plan Template for use in planning and evaluating parent/family involvement activities in each of the standard areas. See box at bottom of this page for detailed instructions on using the plan template and sample plan;

• Parent Survey to help determine the needs and interests of parents in the school community. Completed surveys can help in the development of parent/family involvement activities.

A reproducible promotional flier and order form for the standards booklet and National PTA's book, *Building Successful Partnerships: A Guide for Developing Parent and Family Involvement Programs* is also included in this section. Use it to order additional copies of this booklet, and to order the *Building Successful Partnerships* book.

The parent/family involvement plan template on page 30 can be used by an individual school, a school district, or a state board of education. It is recommended that this template be reproduced and saved in an electronic format for easy updating.

The template should be used to plan and evaluate activities in each of the six National Standards for Parent/Family Involvement Programs. The page should be duplicated as needed for planning in all six standard areas. For each standard list all of the activities that will take place in support of the particular standard, state who will be involved in the activities, what resources will be needed, when the activities will be implemented, and how they will be evaluated. (A sample page of a plan is provided for Standard III: Student Learning.) For activity ideas, consult Action Ideas, beginning on page 12, and PTA Project Ideas, beginning on page 38. The same template should also be used to plan activities in the other sections covered in the parent/family involvement policy (page 27): **Inclusion/Removing Barriers, Professional Development, Implementation, and Evaluation.** All elements of the policy should be addressed in the plan.

Parent/Family Involvement Policy Template

This template is based, in part, on the effective components in various state and local policies. As with any effective policy, the integration and implementation of the contents should be tailored to meet the local needs and circumstances of individual school communities. Use the template as a guide in developing a parent/family involvement policy for your school community.

The phrases in bold type in parentheses identifying the type of statement (e.g., Purpose/Goal Statement, Inclusion Statement, etc.) and supporting statements need not appear in the final policy. **Also, you are to fill in the blanks with the name of your school, school district, or state board of education developing the policy.**

(Purpose/Goal Statement)

_____ understands that engaging parents in the education process is essential to improved academic success for students. It further recognizes that a child's education is a responsibility shared by the school and the family during the entire time a child attends school.
Therefore, _____ shall foster and support active parent involvement so that schools and parents work together as knowledgeable partners in educating children.

(Inclusion Statement)

Although parents may be diverse in culture, language, and needs, they share the school's commitment to the educational success of their children. _____ recognizes its responsibility to eliminate barriers that impede family involvement and to create an environment supportive of comprehensive family involvement programs that have been developed in collaboration with parents. Therefore, this policy shall establish programs and practices that reflect the specific needs of _____ students and their families.

(Elements of Effective Programs Statement)

_____ supports the development, implementation, and regular evaluation of a parent involvement program at _____ that includes parents at all grade levels in a variety of roles. Parent involvement programs will be comprehensive and coordinated in nature. They will include, but not be limited to, the following components of successful parent/family involvement programs based on National PTA's National Standards for Parent/Family Involvement Programs:

- Communication between home and school is regular, two-way, and meaningful. [**Include statements describing the need for a regular exchange of information with families.**]

- Responsible parenting is promoted and supported. [**Include statements explaining the value of recognizing parents as a child's first and most important teacher.**]

- Parents play an integral role in assisting student learning. [**Include statements describing a commitment to giving parents opportunities to participate in their child's learning both at home and at school.**]

- Parents are welcome in the school, and their support and assistance are sought. [**Include statements describing a parent's right to have access to the school, their children's records, and their classroom.**]

- Parents are full partners in the decisions that affect children and families. [**Include statements describing a commitment to providing opportunities for families to share in decisions about school policy and family involvement program design.**]

- Community resources are made available to strengthen school programs, family practices, and student learning. [**Include statements describing a commitment to working with community agencies that provide services to children and families.**]

(Professional Development Statement)

_____ is committed to professional development opportunities for staff and leadership to enhance understanding of effective parent involvement strategies.
_____ also recognizes the importance of administrative leadership in setting expectations and creating a climate conducive to parent participation. [**Include a statement describing a commitment to making opportunities available throughout the school year for professional development in parent involvement.**]

(Commitment to Implementation Statement)

_____ supports the implementation of this policy. A copy of this policy will be distributed to [Mention groups that will receive the policy; for example, all schools, every parent, all teachers…] Support will be provided to parents and teachers as they plan and implement effective parent involvement programs. [Include a statement describing the value of parent input to the design and implementation of the policy. Include a statement describing the importance of committing both time and resources to implementing the contents of the policy.]

(Commitment to Evaluation Statement)

_____ ensures that parents will participate in an evaluation of the content and effect of this policy on student success. The evaluation will be used to improve and/or create practices to enhance parent involvement. [**Include a statement describing how often the policy will be reviewed and revised.**]

Adopted on_____ by_____

[**Include month/day/year**] [**name of school, school district, or state board of education**]

SAMPLE PLAN

Phoebe Apperson Hearst Elementary School
Parent/Family Involvement Plan

Based on National PTA's *National Standards for Parent/Family Involvement Programs*

Standard or Area of Focus: Standard III: Student Learning

Objective: For parents to play a more integral role in assisting student learning at home.

What steps will be taken?	Who will be involved?	What materials/resources or training do we need?	When will it be done?	How will we measure our success?
• Offer a workshop on how parents can support learning and homework at home.	• 2 PTA members • 2–3 teachers	• Teachers and parents to volunteer time to plan the workshop • Location • Speaker • Handouts and workshop evaluation forms • Type of seating/number needed • Possible audiovisual equipment: flip charts, and markers, overhead projector, microphone, podium, TV/VCR • Child care • Translator • Refreshments	October 20, 7:00 p.m.	• Results of workshop evaluations • Increase in completed homework assignments turned in by students
• Create learning kits that guide families to explore an academic area together.	• Teachers • Curriculum coordinator	• Planning time for teachers to create kits and parent/child activities. • Kit contents: list of activities, assignment completion forms that student and parent sign, videos, books, learning toys/games, writing supplies, etc.	• One kit will be taken home per quarter.	• Improved performance on homework and tests by students • Presentations in class • Completion of forms signed by parents and students

Drafted on _____   Adopted on _____   Revised on _____

PLAN TEMPLATE

(Name of School, School District, State Board of Education)
Parent/Family Involvement Plan

Based on National PTA's *National Standards for Parent/Family Involvement Programs*

Standard or Area of Focus: _____

Objective: _____

What steps will be taken?	Who will be involved?	What materials/resources or training do we need?	When will it be done?	How will we measure our success?

Drafted on _____   Adopted on _____   Revised on _____

Parent Survey

PTA needs your help to plan parent involvement programs at our school. Parent involvement is crucial. It helps our children perform better in school. Please take a few minutes to fill out this survey and return it to

1. What specifically would you like to know about the school?

_____

_____

2. From what source do you get most of your information about school? (Check one)

❑ Newsletter   ❑ Friends
❑ Children   ❑ Newspaper
❑ Teachers   ❑ TV
❑ Principal   ❑ Internet/Web
❑ Other _____

3. How effective are the following toward improving communications between your family and the school?

	Good	Fair	Poor
Open houses	❑	❑	❑
Grade-level orientation sessions	❑	❑	❑
Parent-teacher conferences	❑	❑	❑
PTA meetings	❑	❑	❑
School/PTA newsletter	❑	❑	❑

4. As a parent, do you have trouble with any of the following?

	Yes	No	To some degree
Your child's homework	❑	❑	❑
Attending school functions	❑	❑	❑
Spending enough time with your child	❑	❑	❑
Getting in to see your child's teacher(s)	❑	❑	❑
Dealing with your child's problems	❑	❑	❑
Knowing school policies	❑	❑	❑
Motivating your child	❑	❑	❑

5. Would you be interested in attending a class or workshop on how parents can help their children learn?

❑ Yes   ❑ No

6. If you checked "yes" for question 5, please indicate below the types of workshops you would like to participate in to help you help your children learn.

❑ Helping with homework   ❑ Improving reading skills
❑ Improving math skills   ❑ Exploring art
❑ Testing programs and what they mean   ❑ Understanding English-as-a-second-language classes
❑ Helping your child explore career choices
❑ Other _____

7. Would you be interested in attending a class or workshop to enhance your parenting skills?

❑ Yes   ❑ No

8. If you checked "yes" for question 7, please indicate below the types of parenting workshops you'd like to participate in.

❑ Helping your child say NO to drugs
❑ Explaining HIV/AIDS and what to do to protect your child
❑ Gang prevention and my child: Recognizing gang symbols and activities
❑ Teaching children tolerance and to respect differences
❑ Preventing and responding to bullying
❑ Understanding child nutrition and encouraging healthy eating habits
❑ Other _____

9. Where would you like these parenting programs to be held?

❑ In the school   ❑ In a community/public facility   ❑ In the home of a parent in your neighborhood

Would you be willing to host such a session?

❑ Yes   ❑ No

10. When would you like to have these meetings scheduled?
❑ On a week night
❑ In the early morning before school starts
❑ Some time during a weekday
        ❑ Morning   ❑ Afternoon
❑ On a Saturday
        ❑ Morning   ❑ Afternoon   ❑ Evening
❑ On a Sunday
        ❑ Morning   ❑ Afternoon   ❑ Evening

11. Do you agree with the following statements?
I can talk openly with my child's teacher(s).
❑ Yes   ❑ No   ❑ To some degree
I can talk openly with my child's principal.
❑ Yes   ❑ No   ❑ To some degree
I am well-informed by the school or teachers about what my child is doing at school.
❑ Yes   ❑ No   ❑ To some degree
I feel that teachers need to be aware of home problems that may affect my child's work.
❑ Yes   ❑ No   ❑ To some degree

12. Would you like to volunteer in the following areas?
Clerical or administrative duties for school or PTA
❑ Yes   ❑ No
Helping in your child's classroom (e.g., reading aloud, working with individual students)
❑ Yes   ❑ No
Organizing a PTA or school event (e.g., open house, holiday program, cultural arts fair)
❑ Yes   ❑ No
Supervising student events or field trips
❑ Yes   ❑ No
Participating on an advisory committee (on curriculum and textbooks, for example)
❑ Yes   ❑ No
Talking to students about careers or hobbies
❑ Yes   ❑ No
❑ Other _____

13. Check the kinds of resources and services you would like to see made available at the school.
❑ Homework hotline   ❑ Before- or after-school child care
❑ Parent resource center   ❑ Parent support group
❑ Family use of gym, pool, or school library   ❑ School website
❑ E-mail listserv for parents
❑ Other _____

14. I have the following hobbies and work experience that I would be willing to share with the students, school, or PTA:
_____
_____
_____

15. Parent and family involvement at school should be strengthened in the following ways:
_____
_____
_____

Optional (Please complete if you answered "yes" to questions 9 and 12 or answered question 14.)
Name _____
Address _____
Phone _____
Best time to contact _____

Solution Tree

SPECIFICATIONS

- 237 pages
- 6" x 9"
- Grades K–12

WHO IS USING THE BOOK

Building Successful Partnerships: A Guide for Developing Parent and Family Involvement Programs, a comprehensive, practical resource to bring parents, educators, communities, and schools together, has been available since January 31, 2000. Now in its second printing, the book has sold nearly 20,000 copies.

In colleges and universities across the country, the Building Successful Partnerships book is being used to help future educators become aware of the importance of parent/family involvement in education.

University of Alaska, AK
University of Montevallo, AL
Arizona State University, AZ
University of the Pacific, CA
Gevirtz Grad School of Education, CA
Connecticut State University, CT
George Washington University, DC
University of District Columbia, DC
University of Central Florida, FL
Teachers Education Institute, FL
Valdosta State University, GA
Governor's State University, IL
Ball State University, IN
University of Southern Indiana, IN
Manchester College, IN
University of Minnesota, MN
St. Mary's University, MN
College of St. Catherine, MN
University of Akron, OH
Portland State University, OR
Arcadia University, PA
California University, PA
Wayland University, TX
Central Washington University, WA

Solution Tree

(National Educational Service)
304 W. Kirkwood Ave., Suite 2
Bloomington, IN 47404
(800) 733-6786
(812) 336-7790 fax
www.solution-tree.com

Building Successful Partnerships:

A Guide for Developing Parent and Family Involvement Programs
by National PTA

Created for parents, administrators, teachers, parent involvement professionals, Title I coordinators, and leaders of PTAs and other parent groups, **Building Successful Partnerships** helps to facilitate meaningful discussion and provides the foundation for developing quality parent involvement programs that work. The book is based on National PTA's National Standards for Parent/Family Involvement Programs.

The *National Standards for Parent/Family Involvement Programs: An Implementation Guide for School Communities,* is an interactive tool to facilitate discussion, planning, and assessment of parent/family involvement programs. Schools from across the country provide examples of how they implement each of the six standards. A set of assessment questions is included as a guide for school communities to identify strengths and weaknesses in their programs. Reproducible templates are provided to help school teams write parent/family involvement policies and plans.

Publications Order Form

Solution Tree (National Educational Service)
304 W. Kirkwood, Ste. 2
Bloomington, IN 47404
www.solution-tree.com

Item #	Title	Price (1–9 copies)*	Quantity
BKF175	*National Standards for Parent/Family Involvement Programs*	$4.00	_____
BKF095	*Building Successful Partnerships*	$18.95	_____

*Quantity discounts for a single title
10–49 copies . . . . .10% discount
50–99 copies . . . . .20% discount
100 or more copies . . . . .30% discount

Order total _____

Shipping and Handling (Please check one)
❏ Standard orders (within the continental U.S.), 6% of order total + $4.00
❏ Orders outside the continental U.S., 8% of order total + $6.00
❏ Overnight delivery, 20% of order total + $6.00
❏ Two-day delivery, 15% of order total + $6.00
❏ Three-day delivery, 10% of order total + $6.00

Subtotal _____

Grand Total _____

Method of Payment
❏ Check enclosed (payable to Solution Tree)
❏ Purchase order enclosed
(We cannot process your order until we receive an official copy of your purchase order by fax or mail. All purchase orders must be accompanied by a completed order form and must include shipping and handling costs.)
❏ Credit Card (circle one)   Visa   MasterCard   Discover/Novus   American Express

Card# _____   Exp.Date _____

Cardholder Name _____

Cardholder Signature _____
(Your credit card will be charged by Solution Tree.)

Ship to
Name _____

Position _____

Organization _____

Address _____

City/State/ZIP _____

Daytime Phone_____Fax_____E-mail_____

Bill to (if different)
Name _____

Position _____

Organization _____

Address _____

City/State/ZIP _____

Daytime Phone_____Fax_____E-mail_____

Four Easy Ways to Order:

Phone
(800) 733-6786

Fax
(812) 336-7790

Online
www.solution-tree.com

Mail
304 W. Kirkwood Ave.
Suite 2
Bloomington, IN 47404

Other Factors to Consider in Parent/Family Involvement Program Design

When looking at parent/family involvement practices, the following factors should be considered if a school or district is committed to developing its parent/family involvement programs.

Administrative Leadership

The principal or program director plays a pivotal role in making parent and family involvement a reality. Teachers and other staff sense the level of priority administrators give to involving parents. The climate in a school is created, to a large extent, by the tone set in the office of administration. If principals collaborate with parents, teachers will be more likely to follow suit.

Sometimes there is a misperception that partnering with parents, particularly in the decision-making process, will diminish the principal's authority. Yet, the top management models in America are open and collaborative, encouraging subordinates to share their concerns and engaging managers and workers in cooperative problem solving rather than making decisions through strict hierarchical systems.

Such an approach need not diminish the manager's authority, but can lead to better decisions—in businesses or in schools.

Without administrative leadership, long-term progress in family-school partnerships is difficult to achieve since genuine change requires systemic solutions and coordinated efforts with consistent leadership support.

Working together to implement the program standards, principals and teachers can accomplish a great deal. When parent involvement becomes a mutual program goal, and parents, teachers, and administrators work together as a team to develop a plan for reaching the standards, substantial progress results. The principal provides the leadership; the program standards provide the vision.

Affirming Diversity

Programs serving parents and families must be aware and sensitive to the changes in our society represented by the word "diversity." Successful programs increase awareness of all cultures represented. The importance of using translated materials and language interpreters, as needed, cannot be overstated.

We often hear the term "common courtesy," but courtesy is not common; it is culturally determined. The values, attitudes, manners, and views of all populations represented in the community should be respected and honored. The religious holidays and observances of all groups are to be given consideration in the context of the total program serving parents and families.

Not only are programs called upon to serve culturally diverse populations, but the structures and supports for families are continually changing as well. The predominant scenario in most households includes both parents working outside the home. In addition, single-parent families are on the rise as well as the number of grandparents who serve as primary caregivers for their grandchildren. These patterns of change in family structure indicate that the current needs of families are indeed diverse, requiring heightened sensitivity to the increasing demands of home life.

As our society increases in the numbers and groups of diverse populations represented, only those programs willing to be flexible, sensitive, and supportive to the parents, children, and families they serve will be determined effective and worthwhile.

Systemwide Support

Research is clear that parent and family involvement is a wise investment for communities truly concerned about student achievement. If parent involvement traditions and habits are to be transformed, there must be adequate support from the education authorities outside the school.

Proactive parent involvement policies and practices at the district, state, and national levels are prerequisite. From school boards and district offices to state and national departments of education and national professional associations, principals and teachers need to know their leaders are willing to support and encourage them as they seek to implement change.

Supporting parent and family involvement need not be expensive, but financial resources as well as moral support improve chances of success. Support may be in the form of a program coordinator, better access to telephones, or resource center materials to reach out to parents. When policy makers and education leaders make parent involvement a priority, their actions and the support systems they provide reflect their commitment.

Teacher Training in Parent/Family Involvement

Even with the preponderance of research establishing the connection between effective parent involvement and student achievement, few teachers receive solid preparation in how to partner with parents.

Surveys of current practice reveal that

- Most parent involvement preparation occurs in early childhood or special education courses.

- No state requires a separate course in parent involvement for teacher licensure.

- Only a handful of states require parent involvement preparation as part of a course.

- A minority of the states include parent involvement in their competency standards for teachers/administrators or in their standards for teacher/administrator training programs.

- No state requires parent involvement coursework for recertification or renewal of a license.

Still, there are promising signs. National associations that either accredit or set standards for teacher preparation programs support parent involvement as a component in teacher education. The National Council for the Accreditation of Teacher Education (NCATE)'s performance-based system of accreditation of schools, colleges, and departments of education has recently added or strengthened indicators aimed at collaboration with families in its program standards for teacher preparation. The American Association of Colleges for Teacher Education (AACTE) supports parent involvement as an essential component in the preparation of teachers. The National Board for Professional Teacher Standards (NBPTS) has also included family partnership competencies in all of its standards for teacher certification. While each of these efforts could be strengthened, they are, indeed, a step toward improving current practices.

In the meantime, providing teachers with parent and family involvement training and other professional development opportunities becomes critical. The National Standards for Parent/Family Involvement Programs provide a good basis for this preparation, indicating what practices lead to quality. Teachers should also be familiar with the research base and focus on communication and interpersonal skills, particularly those that help parents feel comfortable and respected.

The use of mentoring, peer coaching, mini-presentations with follow-up, and other collaborative methods for professional development suit this topic very well. Rather than waiting for teachers to take special courses or providing a one-time training, schools and programs should provide information on positive practices while offering opportunities for staff feedback and evaluation.

Aside from the benefits of increased student performance, effective parent and family involvement provides teachers with a much-needed support system. Research indicates that schools that work well with families have improved teacher/staff morale and have higher ratings of teachers by parents.

PTA Project Ideas

When planning PTA activities, consider projects in each of the six standards to ensure a comprehensive approach to parent involvement. PTA projects should supplement and enhance those sponsored by the school. Some projects or activities may address more than one standard, such as a project that addresses parenting skills and student learning, or a project that combines volunteering and collaborating with community. Keep in mind, too, that in selecting activities, they should be in keeping with the objectives identified in the school's parent/family involvement plan.

Communicating

Promote parent/teacher conferences by conducting support activities. In consultation with school staff, develop a **Preparing for Parent-Teacher Conferences publication** or flier with sample questions to assist parents in partnering with teachers. If your school offers evening conferences, consider sponsoring a free or low-cost meal to enable parents to come right after work. Distribute calendars for recording upcoming student events, assignments, and dates when parents should check back with teachers on student progress. Assist parents who attend conferences to find classrooms, counseling offices, and support materials.

Offer to design and print Happy Grams for teachers to report positive behavior or achievement to parents. Consider covering mailing costs if necessary.

Participate in the development of a Parent Handbook that meets the needs of parents and encourages active participation. Promote the handbook with parents, highlighting examples of the important information in the book in school newsletters and other forms of home-school communication.

Publicize the hours when administrators and teachers are available for parent visits and any procedures for contacting teachers on the telephone or in writing. Promote use of these opportunities for discussing children's progress.

Advocate before-school policy makers regarding the need for staff to have adequate access to telephones and other means of communication. If your school has an automated homework hotline or other parent information system, promote its use among parents.

Build a PTA or school website to reach parents that you may not otherwise have access to in your community to increase communication between home and school. National PTA has partnered with Family Education Network to provide schools the tools they need. Log on to www.pta.org/ptacommunity to find out more.

Appoint a PTA newsletter chair or committee to work with the school to **help produce or contribute to the school newsletter** to make it relevant, useful, and timely for parents. Include a two-way communication mechanism in the school newsletter such as a question-and-answer section or a mini-survey in each edition. In secondary schools, encourage mailing of the newsletter directly to parents.

At a Back-to-School Event and/or a faculty meeting, present a **"How to Partner" role play of a parent-teacher conference** where parents and teachers share information and plan for the future. For more ideas on conducting a back-to-school event, visit www.pta.org/parentinvolvement/bts/index.asp.

Parenting

Sponsor regular parenting classes or an **annual Parent University** in cooperation with local professionals. Provide child care and transportation if possible. Consider seeking donations for a **Toy Lending Library** where parents can check out an age-appropriate toy for their child when the class is over.

Host a **VIP (Very Important Parent) column** in the school's newsletter to highlight parent tips, show real-life examples of how to handle parenting challenges, and provide general information for parents. The newsletter might also include a tear-off form for submitting questions to be answered by a parenting professional in a "Dear _____" column.

Distribute parenting information at parent-teacher conferences.

Host a **weekend parents' breakfast** where teachers and school administrators prepare and serve a meal to parents and children. After breakfast, hold roundtable discussions on important parenting issues while providing a separate activity for children.

Start a parent book club. Advertise the current selection, give parents a chance to meet to discuss it, or just include excerpts in the school newsletter.

Establish a family resource center with a broad array of materials and information for parents. Local businesses and agencies are often willing to help fund this kind of project. Convene a committee to oversee the development, operation, and review of the center.

Host activities at the school that bring parents and children together, from **Lunch Buddies** where parents can drop in to eat lunch with children to inviting parents to sit with their child during school assemblies.

Create **"Together Grams,"** a half-sheet flier with one activity idea for parents to do with their children, such as "Talk to your children about when you were their age." On the back, provide information about why the activity is valuable for kids and how it supports academic learning.

Student Learning

Sponsor a "Parents Make the Difference" evening where parents can get an overview of what students will be learning, how students will be assessed, what parents should expect, and how they can assist and make a difference. These could be for an individual class, grade level, or subject area. At the secondary level, these events might focus around a particular academic discipline, such as Science Achievement Night. Teachers from various courses—biology or chemistry—would conduct sessions giving tips about how to excel in

---

Building Partnerships to Promote Student Success

To increase your school's awareness of parent/family involvement on children's academic success, call on PTA to present a **Building Successful Partnerships** workshop at your school. Request a workshop on

- Putting the National Standards for Parent/Family Involvement Programs into Action
- Working with Teachers and Administrators
- Forming School Teams, Creating Policies, and Developing Action Plans
- Parenting/How To Help Your Child Succeed
- Schools of Excellence Certification

To request a workshop in your area, contact your state PTA office. State contact information can be found at www.pta.org/aboutpta/stoffice.asp.

their particular class. (Be sure to make it clear what parents will receive and how their participation will enhance student achievement.)

Following the first report card period, **sponsor study skills sessions** where parents come with their students to learn how to improve grades and study habits. Specifying that a parent should attend with the student tends to increase the influence of these sessions.

Include a "Did You Know?" column in each school or PTA newsletter, highlighting the research in the *National Standards for Parent/Family Involvement Programs* booklet on how parent involvement affects student success. When parents understand the value of their participation, they're much more likely to get involved.

If your school uses portfolio reviews as part of student assessment, **offer to assist teachers in organizing portfolio reviews** as part of parent-teacher conference night. The PTA could promote the event, contact parents, and arrange the logistics for these sessions. Teachers would conduct the review sessions.

Host a College and Career Fair. Invite businesses and local people representing a variety of careers to attend and provide information about available employment opportunities. Ask postsecondary guidance and financial aid counselors, as well as presidents of student organizations to talk to students about what to expect in college. Information might include how to make course choices, apply for financial aid, join social or academic clubs, seek campus employment, and look for housing.

Offer to provide funds or seek donations to **create Exploration Kits** that support teachers' activities in an academic subject area. The kits can contain a list of activities, related videos, books, writing supplies, learning toys, or games that provide ideas and ways for parents and children to explore an academic subject together. Teachers could circulate the kits among the students or make them available at parent-teacher conferences for parents to check out.

Sponsor academic events, such as **Science Fairs or Geography Bees.** Be sure to remind parents how they can support their child's learning through participating in such events.

Publicize ways parents can support student learning. Have students create posters or signs to display in the halls during parent-teacher conferences with tips for parents. Get

Supporting Teachers Supports Student Learning

Make Teacher Appreciation Week an annual event for your PTA, school, and community. Whether you create recognition awards, hold a special event, or ask local businesses to "adopt" a teacher, it's your chance to promote teachers' hard work, dedication, and involvement. Prior to the week, ask teachers to complete the phrase, "If I had only one wish, it would be..." Provide supplies and volunteers to help each class create a mural that describes and depicts each teacher's wish.

This program promotes

1. Home-school cooperation and student learning;

2. Volunteering opportunities and support of teachers; and

3. Involvement and collaboration with the entire community.

For more ideas on honoring teachers, go to www.pta.org/taw.

the local newspaper to run articles with specific suggestions for parent involvement. Look for creative methods to get the message out and get parents involved.

Volunteering

In cooperation with the school administration, conduct a school climate survey. Is your school's climate sunny and friendly to parents? Or is it fair to partly cloudy? Use the information received to guide efforts to make the school's climate more inviting.

Host a "How You Can Make a Difference" orientation session for parents and volunteers each year. Invite school staff to address relevant topics, demonstrate equipment use, and provide parents and other volunteers with a packet of timely information.

Create a volunteer center in the school. While it may take creativity, almost any facility can accommodate some sort of welcoming area for volunteers, from a corner of the library to an area in a hallway with a couple of lockers for personal belongings. Put up a bulletin board for announcements, and be sure there is a place to sign in and record volunteer hours.

Show appreciation. Thank volunteers throughout the year, in the school newsletter, at special events, and using personal thank-you notes. **Consider creating a Wall of Fame display** or bulletin board with pictures of volunteers helping with school activities and events. Showing what and how much can be accomplished by volunteers can encourage others to get involved.

Create volunteer opportunities that go beyond traditional tasks that volunteers perform. For example, at the secondary level, consider a **Parents in the Halls Program**, which encourages parents to drop in and get their exercise walking at the high school, instead of at the gym. After picking up a volunteer badge at the office, these parents perform an important service by increasing the adult presence in the building and thereby reducing behavior problems. As a side benefit, parents get acquainted with the school.

Publish a Volunteer Resource Book, listing the interests and availability of volunteers for school staff members' use. Survey parents regarding their interests, so volunteer work will be meaningful. Be sure to determine how frequently a volunteer would like to participate, including the option of just one time per year. Include options for those who are available to help at home. Use the resource book to help match school needs with volunteer interests.

Recruit one room representative for each classroom who would be responsible for coordinating volunteer activities for the class. This person would work closely with the teacher in matching interests and needs.

Publicize the contributions of volunteers. Tally the hours given over the course of the year and present the school with a symbolic check for the value of the service.

School Decision Making and Advocacy

Facilitate parent participation on school committees and other community groups, such as a city council. Advertise committee assignments well in advance and actively recruit representatives. Where possible, elect those who will be representing the PTA and find ways for them to report to the membership. One school calls its parent program **Partners for Progress,** and the participants are invited to report on their progress at each PTA meeting.

Continually **seek out parent perspectives** and input by including a mini-poll (one question) in each school newsletter and providing a space for feedback. Set up a special voice mailbox at your school or e-mail box to receive feedback from your mini-polls.

Frequently **publish the school's process for resolving parent concerns:** how to define the problem, whom to approach first, how to develop solutions, and so forth. Encourage parents to address problems early before they grow.

Sponsor an Advocate Training Program where parents learn how to advocate effectively for their children in school situations such as parent-teacher conferences, at school board meetings, and in public forums where decisions are being made that affect children.

In cooperation with the school administration, **sponsor a school accountability meeting** where school officials describe school programs, services, and performance data. Following these presentations, parents, staff, and community members discuss the information received and make suggestions for future goal setting. As an annual tradition, this becomes a process for continuous improvement.

Encourage Parents to Join National PTA's Member-to-Member Network

The Member-to-Member network is the grassroots advocacy system that provides direct contact by PTA members with members of Congress, and occasionally with federal regulatory agencies. When such contact is needed, National PTA's Washington, DC, Office issues Action Alerts describing pending legislative issues and action needed. Network participants also have access to a staff liaison that can answer questions and otherwise assist in advocacy efforts.

Sign up today at the "PTA and Washington" section of National PTA's website at www.pta.org.

Encourage the school to **develop a Student Advocacy Handbook** with information about how parents can participate more effectively as partners with students and the school. Include the process for resolving concerns, ways to improve parent-teacher conferences, tips for good study habits, how to develop cooperative relationships, and so forth.

Sponsor seminars to inform high school parents about how to be involved in the decisions affecting course selection, career planning, and preparation for postsecondary opportunities. These seminars could be for particular age groups (e.g., Freshman Orientation Luncheon or Sophomore Night), or for particular topics (e.g., Preparing for College Entrance Exams or College Expo).

Work with students, parents, teachers, school administrators, community leaders, and businesses to **develop a parent/family involvement policy** to establish the vision, common mission, and foundation for parent/family involvement programs in your community.

Collaborating with Community

Host an annual Health Fair. Using a carnival-like atmosphere, community health providers host booths and workshops to inform parents and teens about student health topics and available services. Invite local hospital personnel or paramedics to provide demonstrations of emergency care or safety techniques.

Host an annual Book Fair. Activities can include author talks, storytelling, a used book exchange/sale, a puppet show, literary costume contest, games that promote literature or reading skills, create-your-own-book activity, or a library card sign-up drive. Invite local businesses or bookstores to sponsor the event.

Contact alumni from the school to **participate in an Alumni Sponsors Program.** School alumni would be asked to volunteer time or make a donation to the school.

Bring the school and the community into the workplace with student performances or community service fairs held at different times during the day. Businesses can also sponsor community resource workshops for teachers during the summer to help them learn about the educational, cultural, and business resources in the community.

Sponsor an annual Give Back Day where students go out into the community to perform needed work or services. Coordinate your student activities with local authorities, a chamber of commerce, or city council to find the most appropriate and beneficial services that students might give back to the community.

Offer PTA volunteers to assist a chamber of commerce or community group in one of its annual events or programs. Your PTA's involvement in community activities can help build goodwill and support for your PTA and its activities.

Phoebe Apperson Hearst–National PTA Excellence in Education Partnership Award

This award program recognizes PTAs whose collaborative efforts with parents, families, educators, and community members promote parent/family involvement with ongoing programs that encourage student success. Based on the National Standards for Parent/Family Involvement Programs, this award provides PTAs with an opportunity to receive national recognition as well as to share their outstanding programs with other PTAs. For more information on this award, go to www.pta.org/parentinvolvement/awards/index.asp.

Involve senior citizens in volunteer projects and programs. Host an open house at a local senior citizen center to recruit volunteers. You may want to organize a **Senior Volunteer Day,** where once a month seniors are invited into the school to assist as hall/lunch monitors, library assistants, or reading tutors. For secondary schools, you could start a **Senior-to-Senior Program,** where high school seniors would host senior citizens coming into the school to share life or work experiences as a part of a social science or history class.

Ask the local newspaper or community newsletter editor to **include reminders about upcoming parent events.** Provide facts about the importance and impact of parent involvement on student success and request employer cooperation in allowing parents to attend parent-teacher conferences.

Develop paycheck-size cards with **tips for how parents can foster their child's success.** Contact employers about including the cards with employee paychecks.

Reflecting the Standards

One very successful and popular PTA program that addresses all six of the standards for parent and family involvement programs is National PTA's **Reflections Program.** Each year, the National PTA Reflections Program recognizes outstanding student works in literature, musical composition, photography, and visual arts. The Reflections Program encourages and promotes

1. Home-school communication and cooperation
2. Parent participation and support of arts in education
3. Student learning and expression through the arts
4. Volunteering and leadership opportunities
5. Arts advocacy and arts in education awareness
6. Involvement and collaboration with the entire community

Over the past 35 years, more than 12 million students, along with their parents, schools, and communities, have participated in the program through local PTAs. Contact your state PTA for information on starting a Reflections Program for your PTA.

Bibliography

Following is a list of current and relevant studies cited in or used to develop this guide. These materials can also be used by parents, teachers, and administrators as they research parent involvement program development.

America Goes Back to School: Get Involved! Stay Involved!: Information for Families and Community Members. (2000). Washington, DC: U.S. Department of Education, Partnership for Family Involvement in Education: Office of Educational Research and Improvement, Educational Resources Information Center.

Berger, E. H. (2004). *Parents as Partners in Education: Families and Schools Working Together.* Upper Saddle River, NJ: Merrill.

A Call to Commitment: Fathers' Involvement in Children's Learning. (2000). Jessup, MD: U.S. Department of Education.

Canter, L., and Canter, M. (2001). *Parents on Your Side: A Teacher's Guide to Creating Positive Relationships with Parents.* Los Angeles: Canter & Associates.

Christenson, S., and Sheridan, S. M. (2001). *Schools and Families: Creating Essential Connections for Learning.* New York: Guilford Press.

Dickinson, S. B. (2001). *Children First: ABCs of School Success: A Guide for Parents.* Lanham, MD: Scarecrow Press

Dodd, A. W., and Konzal, J. L. (2000). *Making Our High Schools Better: How Parents and Teachers Can Work Together.* New York: St. Martin's Press.

Dodd, A. W., and Konzal, J. L. (2002). *How Communities Build Stronger Schools: Stories, Strategies, and Promising Practices for Educating Every Child.* New York: Palgrave.

Epstein, J. L. (2001). *School, Family, and Community Partnerships: Preparing Educators, and Improving Schools.* Boulder, CO: Westview Press.

Epstein, J. L. (2002). *School, Family, and Community Partnerships: Your Handbook for Action.* Thousand Oaks, CA: Corwin Press.

Epstein, J. L., Sanders, M. G., and Clark, L. A. (1999). *Preparing Educators for School-Family-Community Partnerships: Results of a National Survey of Colleges and Universities.* Baltimore, MD: Center for Research on the Education of Students Placed at Risk, Johns Hopkins University and Howard University; Washington, DC: U.S. Department of Education, Office of Educational Research and Improvement, Educational Resources Information Center.

Family Involvement in Children's Education: Successful Local Approaches: An Idea Book. (2001). Washington, DC: Office of Educational Research and Improvement, U.S. Department of Education.

Gestwicki, C. (2004). *Home, School, and Community Relations: A Guide to Working with Families.* Australia; Clifton Park, NY: Thomson/Delmar Learning.

Henderson, A. T. (2001). *Community Organizing for School Reform, Washington, DC: A Recovering Plantation.* New York: New York University, New York Institute for Education and Social Policy. (ERIC Document Reproduction Service No. ED 469535)

Henderson, A. T. (2002). *No Child Left Behind: What's in It for Parents.* Arlington, VA: Parent Leadership Associates.

Henderson, A. T., Mapp, K. L., and Averett, A. (2002). *A New Wave of Evidence: The Impact of School, Family, and Community Connections on Student Achievement.* Austin, TX: National Center for Family & Community Connections with Schools.

Lueder, D. C. (2000). *Creating Partnerships with Parents: An Educator's Guide.* Lanham, MD. Scarecrow Press.

Mariconda, B. (2003). *Easy and Effective Ways to Communicate with Parents.* New York: Scholastic Professional Books.

Martínez, Y. G., and Velázquez, J. A. (2000). *Involving Migrant Families in Education.* Charleston, WV: Clearinghouse on Rural Education and Small Schools, Appalachia Educational Laboratory.

National PTA. (2000). *Building Successful Partnerships: A Guide for Developing Parent and Family Involvement Programs.* Bloomington, IN: National Educational Service.

Nord, C. W., Brimhall, D., and West, J. (1997). *Fathers' Involvement in Their Children's Schools.* Washington, DC: U.S. Department of Education, Office of Educational Research and Improvement, National Center for Education Statistics.

Olsen, G. W., and Fuller, M. L. (2003). *Home-School Relations: Working Successfully with Parents and Families.* Boston: Allyn and Bacon.

Sanders, M. G., and Epstein, J. L. (1998). *School-Family-Community Partnerships in Middle and High Schools: From Theory to Practice.* Baltimore: Center for Research on the Education of Students Placed at Risk, Johns Hopkins University and Howard University; Washington, DC: U.S. Department of Education, Office of Educational Research and Improvement, Educational Resources Information Center.

Sanders, M. G., and Epstein, J. L., and Connors-Tadros, L. (1999) *Family Partnerships with High Schools: The Parents' Perspective.* Baltimore: Center for Research on the Education of Students Placed at Risk, Johns Hopkins University and Howard University; Washington, DC: U.S. Department of Education, Office of Educational Research and Improvement, Educational Resources Information Center.

Trumbull, E. (2001). *Bridging Cultures Between Home and School: A Guide for Teachers* (special focus on immigrant Latino families). Mahwah, NJ: L. Erlbaum Associates.

Additional Support

For additional copies of the **National Standards for Parent/Family Involvement Programs booklet,** which are available through Solution Tree (National Educational Service), use the order form on page 34.

National PTA's book, *Building Successful Partnerships: A Guide for Developing Parent/Family Involvement Programs,* can also be ordered for **$18.95** from Solution Tree, (item# BKF095). To place an order for the book use the order form on page 34.

Schools, PTAs, or other institutions can request a **Building Successful Partnerships** workshop, which builds awareness of the benefits of parent involvement and provides help in implementing the standards. Go to www.pta.org/parentinvolvement/bsp/training.asp to request a workshop.

For more information on parent involvement, including ideas from PTAs across the country on how they implement parent/family involvement programs, become a subscriber to *Our Children,* National PTA's magazine. To view a sample issue and subscribe, go to www.pta.org/aboutpta/store/oc_magazine.asp.

Acknowledgments

Nearly 100 national education, health, and parent involvement groups have endorsed the National Standards for Parent/Family Involvement Programs. National PTA thanks the following organizations and institutions for agreeing to uphold these standards.

Academy for Educational Development
www.aed.org

Afterschool Alliance
www.afterschoolalliance.org

After-School Corporation
www.tascorp.org

American Academy of Pediatrics
www.aap.org

American Association of Colleges for Teacher Education
www.aacte.org

American Association of School Administrators
www. aasa.org

American Association of School Librarians/ Young Adult Library Services Association (YALSA)
www.ala.org/aasl

American Federation of Teachers
www.aft.org

American School Counselor Association
www.schoolcounselor.org

American School Food Service Association
www.asfsa.org

American School Health Association
www.ashaweb.org

Anti-Defamation League
www.adl.org

Arts Education Partnership
www.aep-arts.org

The ASPIRA Association, Inc.
www.aspira.org

Association for Childhood Education International
www.acei.org

Association for Supervision and Curriculum Development
www.ascd.org

Association of State and Territorial Health Officials
www.astho.org

Baldwin Wallace College, Division of Education
www.bw.edu

Cable in the Classroom
www.ciconline.com

Center for Law and Education
www.cleweb.org

Center on School, Family, and Community Partnerships at Johns Hopkins University
www.csos.jhu.edu

Central Connecticut State University, School of Education & Professional Studies
www.education.ccsu.edu

Coalition for Community Schools
www.communityschools.org

Community Solutions International
www.community-solutions.com.au

Council for Exceptional Children
www.cec.sped.org

Council of Chief State School Officers
www.ccsso.org

Council of the Great City Schools
www.cgcs.org

Department of Defense Education Activity
www.odedodea.edu

Education Collaborative of Washoe County, Inc.
www.washoe.k12.nv.us

Family Education Network
www.familyeducation.com

Family Support America
www.familysupportamerica.org

Howard University Graduate Programs in Urban School Psychology
www.howard.edu

Institute for Responsive Education
www.responsiveeducation.org

International Reading Association
www.ira.org

MegaSkills Education Center of the Home and School Institute
www.megaskillshsi.org

National Alliance of Black School Educators
www.nabse.org

National Art Education Association
www.naea-reston.org

National Association for Gifted Children
www.nagc.org

National Association for Music Education
www.menc.org

National Association of Elementary School Principals
www.naesp.org

National Association of Multicultural Education
www.nameorg.org

National Association of School Nurses
www.nasn.org

National Association of School Psychologists
www.naspweb.org

National Association of Secondary School Principals
www.nassp.org

National Association of State Boards of Education
www.nasbe.org

National Association of State Directors of Special Education, Inc.
www.nasdse.org

National Association of State Directors of Vocational Technical Education Consortium
www.careertech.org

National Black Child Development Institute, Inc.
www.nbcdi.org

National Board for Professional Teaching Standards
www.nbpts.org

National Center for Community Education
www.nccenet.org

National Center for Family Literacy
www.famlit.org/index.cfm

National Coalition for Parent Involvement in Education
www.ncpie.org

National Coalition of Title I/Chapter 1 Parents
www.nctic1p.org

National Community Education Association
www.ncea.com

National Council for Accreditation of Teacher Education
www.ncate.org

National Council of La Raza
www.nclr.org

National Council on Family Relations
www.ncfr.org

National Crime Prevention Council
www.ncpc.org/

National Dropout Prevention Center
www.dropoutprevention.org

National Education Association
www.nea.org

National Fatherhood Initiative
www.fatherhood.org

National Head Start Association
www.nhsa.org

National Information Center for Children and Youth with Disabilities
www.nichcy.org

National Middle School Association
www.nmsa.org

National Practitioners Network for Fathers and Families, Inc.
www.npnff.org

National School Boards Association
www.nsba.org

National University
www.nu.edu

National Urban League
www.nul.org

North Central Regional Educational Laboratory
www.ncrel.org

Nova Southeastern University, Graduate School of Education
www.nova.edu

Parent Educational Advocacy Training Center
www.peatc.org

The Parent Institute
www.par-inst.com

Parents As Teachers National Center, Inc.
www.patnc.org

Parents for Public Schools, Inc.
www.parents4publicschools.com

The Policy Institute for Family Impact Seminars
www.uwex.edu/ces/familyimpact

Portland State University, Graduate School of Education
www.ed.pdx.edu

Project Parents, Inc.
www.projectparents.org

RMC Research Corporation
www.rmcdenver.com

Satellite Education Resources Consortium
www.SERC.org

South Carolina School Improvement Council
www.ed.sc.edu/sic/

Teachers College, University of Nebraska – Lincoln
http://tc.unl.edu/

Terrel H. Bell School Reform Network
www.bellschoolnetwork.org

University of Alaska Southeast Center for Teacher Education
www.uas.alaska.edu

University of Hawaii, College of Education
www.hawaii.edu

Wayne State University, College of Education
www.coe.wayne.edu

Webster's International
www.bowdoinmethod.com

National Standards
for Parent/Family Involvement Programs

National PTA®

every child. *one* voice.®

Revised 2004

Project Director, Rosalee Gentile
Project Editor, Joan Kuersten
Contributing Editor, Lorenza DiNatale
Proofreader, Mark Bennett
Design Manager, Dana McMurray